Holy Mackerel
a fish story about a little misunderstanding

written and illustrated by Skip Ploss

2nd Edition
copyright © 2008, 2015 Richard E "Skip" Ploss
http://www.plossville.com
Published By ElectricBruin Creative
www.electricbruin.com
No Portion of this book my be reproduced for any purpose
without the written consent of the author.
ISBN-13: 978-1515348054
ISBN-10: 1515348059

for

the students and staff of Miller and Driscoll Schools Wilton Connecticut 2007-2008
including Mrs. Casl's 2nd Grade Class and Mrs. McGann's 1st Grade Class.

for Laura and Sarah

finally

for Carol,
whose exclaimation of "Holy Mackerel"
caused this book to pop "fully formed" into my head
one afternoon in March 2008.

> "Do you mean me?"
>
> James Mavor Morell
> a character in a play called
> **Candida**

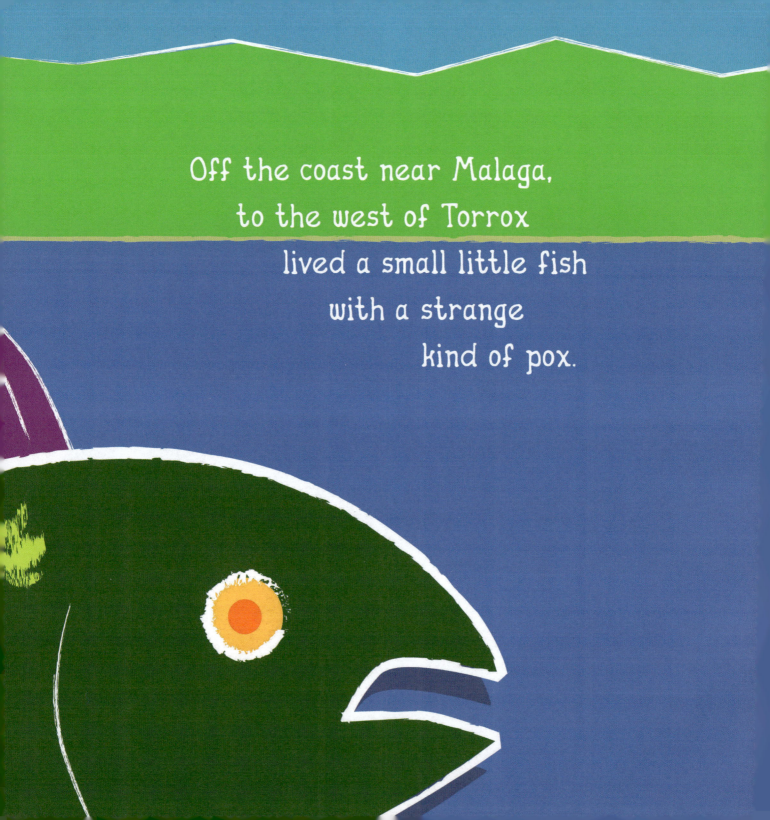

Mack was a Mackerel
   but a Mackerel with holes.
Other fish would call to him,
   "Hey! how'd you get those?"

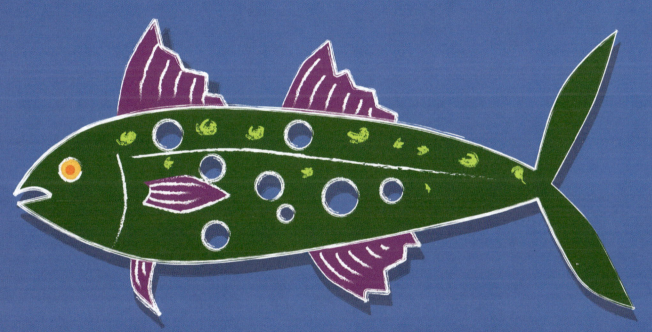

But Mack didn't know, he had never been told.
   He had always had holes
      since he was just a day old.

But none seemed to care
thus the constant barrage
of questions and comments.
"Was it weird camouflage?"

Then one day a barnacle,
on the keel of a boat,
called him a new name
as by Mack he did float.

Holy Mackerel!

He called as his boat drifted by.

And that was the start.
From then on all the same
When he'd meet a new fish
then they'd too yell the name.

Holy Mackerel!

Holy Mackerel!

They'd yell and they'd shout,
he'd feel really sad and he'd sniffle or pout.

Mack would slowly swim off
and the yelling would fade.

Holy Mackerel!

Holy Mackerel

He'd hide in
a shipwreck,
a crab trap
or cave.

sigh

This went on year after year
off the south coast of Spain
and Mack began showing
clear signs of the strain.

His eyes were all red,
his gill slits were frayed,
his tail was in tatters
Mom and Dad were dismayed.

"It's my holes...

Mack began....

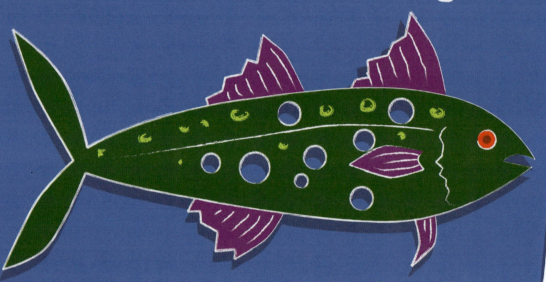

they're not normal, not right, other fish call me names it's not kind or polite.

"Ah, son, you're just different, as different can be there's no one just like you anywhere in the sea."

That's great Dad. Mack thought, unbelieving and weary, a Branzino swam by and asked...

"What's the fuss deary?"

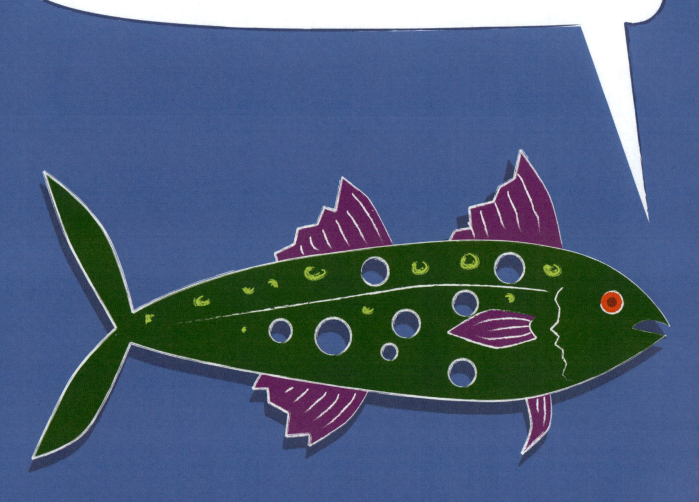

"There's a name that they call me

said Mack to the Branzino
whose, name it turned out, was Louise Zinotino.

Louise seemed to ask questions
from a genuine knowledge.
You see she'd been a journalism student in college.

I understand why...

...you pout and you fret,
I know why they do it.
You should not be upset
You see, here's the thing,
Holy Mackerel's a saying
folks use when surprised
by something cool or amazing.

I think that it's just
that they're wowed by your look,
That despite all your holes
you can read, you can cook.

You are who you are
and there's no one quite like you.
I bet they're amazed
at the things that you *can* do.

And so thats what he did.
He went out to the fish
and suggested a new term.
They complied with his wish.

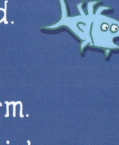

So the next time they saw
something cool or amazing
they said "Holy Cow"
as a new kind of phrasing.

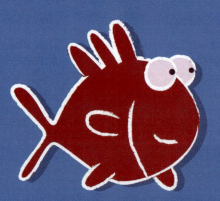

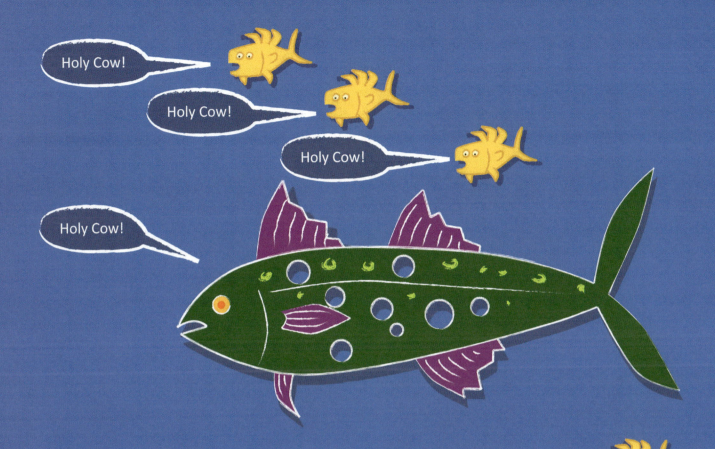

Mack was happy, elated
and his friends were as well.
That should have ended the problem
but it did not, sad to tell.

For each time that they said it
their voices would ride

bubbles up to the surface then out on the tide....

Then picked up by trade winds
they'd float by Gibraltar,
across the Atlantic
and a town by the water.

Then over the mountains and the great plains beyond. To a farm south of Enid under a tree by a pond.

And there in the shade stood an old Guernsey cow,

Made in the USA
Charleston, SC
14 December 2016